Oscar Browning, John Milton

Milton's tractate on Education

Oscar Browning, John Milton

Milton's tractate on Education

ISBN/EAN: 9783337058371

Printed in Europe, USA, Canada, Australia, Japan

Cover: Foto ©ninafisch / pixelio.de

More available books at **www.hansebooks.com**

𝔓itt 𝔓ress 𝔖eries.

MILTON'S

TRACTATE ON EDUCATION.

A FACSIMILE REPRINT FROM THE EDITION
OF 1673.

EDITED WITH AN INTRODUCTION AND NOTES

BY

OSCAR BROWNING, M.A.

FELLOW AND LECTURER OF KING'S COLLEGE, CAMBRIDGE, AND
FORMERLY ASSISTANT MASTER AT ETON COLLEGE.

𝔠ambridge:
AT THE UNIVERSITY PRESS.
1890

TO

JAMES WARD,

FELLOW OF TRINITY COLLEGE, CAMBRIDGE,

THIS BOOK IS DEDICATED.

PREFACE.

MILTON's Tractate on Education has been a favourite study of mine for five and twenty years. When I first went as an assistant master to a large public school, about the time when the Public Schools Commission was beginning to sit, it occurred to me as an ardent educational reformer, that a cheap reprint of Milton's Tractate would have a good effect in clearing the thoughts and opinions of my colleagues and others on the pressing question of the day. I had opened negotiations with the school bookseller for executing a reprint which I intended to scatter broadcast in pamphlet form through the public schools of England. My theories received a rude shock. One of the senior masters at my school set Milton as a subject for a Latin theme to his division, and told his boys that they were to prove that Milton, like Burke, went mad in his old age. I had never heard of this idea before, and I asked the master on what grounds it rested. He replied, "Did he not write a crack-brained book about education in his old age?" Milton was by no means in his old age when he wrote the Tractate, but that did not matter. I concluded that my scheme would be useless, and gave it up.

I am now able to carry out the design formed so long ago, under more favourable auspices. Milton's Tractate is a subject set in the Teachers' Certificate Examination of the University of Cambridge for the present year. As far as I am aware, no separate reprint of the work exists, and it therefore became necessary to prepare one.

The present edition is an exact facsimile of the edition of 1673, published in Milton's lifetime. I have carried the accuracy of the facsimile so far as even to reproduce Milton's misprints. I have done this because it would have in some cases spoilt the appearance and the arrangement of the pages to have corrected them, while in no case are they likely to cause any difficulty to the reader. They are all, I believe, mentioned in the notes. The notes have been confined to what appeared to be necessary for the explanation of the text. I have edited the work as a schoolmaster, and not as a philological student of the English language. By the kindness of Messrs C. K. Paul, Trench and Co. I am able to reprint as an Introduction the account which I had given of Milton's Tractate in the sixth chapter of my *Introduction to the History of Educational Theories*[1].

---

[1] *An Introduction to the History of Educational Theories*, by Oscar Browning, M.A. London : Kegan Paul, Trench and Co.

INTRODUCTION.

THE tractate of John Milton is written in the form of a letter to Mr Samuel Hartlib, the son of a Polish merchant who resided mainly in London. He was a friend of every new discovery which seemed likely to advance the happiness of the human race. He took great interest in science, in the union of the Protestant Churches, and above all in education. He published in 1651, 'Propositions for the Erecting of a College of Husbandry Learning,' or, in modern phraseology, an agricultural college, in which he proposed that apprentices, received at the age of fifteen, should after seven years' instruction receive money to set themselves up in a farm, and a yearly payment for four years. Also in 1647, Sir William Petty, the founder of the Lansdowne family, wrote to Mr Hartlib a letter containing a scheme for a trade or industrial school, a grand plan which we may possibly see realised in our own day by the establishment of a technological university in London. Sir William Petty says, 'All apprentices might learn the theory of their trades before they are bound to a master, and consequently be exempted from the tedium of a seven years' bondage, and having spent but about three years with a master, may spend the other four in travelling to learn breeding and the perfection of their trades.' To the same category belongs Cowley's scheme of a philosophical college, published in 1661, the school part of which bears so much resemblance to Milton's scheme as to make it certain that Cowley in writing it must have had the former in his mind. Although these plans were never carried out, being indeed impossible in the troubled times of the Commonwealth and ill suited to the frivolous temper of the Restoration, they shew us plainly enough the desire which was fermenting in men's minds for a better and more liberal education. Had they met with more success the English might have been by this time the best educated nation in Europe.

It was natural that Hartlib should have been specially attracted by the writings of Comenius, the great Moravian teacher, who announced to his age a discovery as important as that of Bacon, heralded with the same confidence, and promising as great results. We have seen that one of the most important points on which Comenius insists is the simultaneous teaching of words and things. Endless time had been spent on the mere routine of language—why not at least attempt to utilise this labour, and while the drudgery of words and sentences is proceeding, take care that what is

learnt is worth remembering for itself. We shall
find these same lines of thought running through
Milton's tractate. Writing to Mr Hartlib, he
proceeds to set down 'that voluntary idea, which
hath long in silence presented itself to me, of a
better education in extent and comprehension far
more large, and yet of time far shorter and of
attainment far more certain than have yet been
in practice.' He asks his friend 'to accept these
few observations which have flowered off, and
are as it were the burnishings of many studious
and contemplative years altogether spent in the
search of civil and religious knowledge, and since
it pleased you so well in the relating, I here give
you them to dispose of.'

Milton begins by the principle that the end of
learning is to repair the sins of our first parents by
regaining to know God aright; and, because God
can only be known in His works, we must by the
knowledge of sensible things arrive gradually at
the contemplation of the insensible and invisible.
Now we must begin with language; but language
is only the instrument conveying to us things
useful to be known. No man can be called
learned who does not know the solid things in
languages as well as the languages themselves.
Here we see asserted the important principle that
words and things must go together, and that
things are more important than words. The next
principle with which we are familiar in the writings
of Comenius and others, is that we must proceed

from the easier to the more difficult. We are warned against 'a preposterous exaction, forcing the empty wits of children to compose themes, verses, and orations, which are the acts of the ripest judgment.' Matters were indeed far worse in Milton's time than they are now in this respect. We have to a great extent thrown off the tyranny of the grammarians and the schoolmen. But we are still guilty of the 'error of misspending our prime youth at the schools and universities either in learning mere words or such things chiefly as were better unlearnt.' We have still as much need as ever that someone should 'point us out the right path of a virtuous and noble education, so laborious indeed at first ascent, but else so smooth, so green, and so full of goodly prospects and melodious sounds on every side that the harp of Orpheus was not more charming.'

Milton defines what he means by education in the following words : ' I call a complete and generous education that which fits a man to perform justly, skilfully, and magnanimously all the offices, both public and private, of peace and war.' To attain this object, first a spacious house and grounds about it is to be found, fit for an academy to lodge about 130 students under the government of one head. This is to be both school and university, to give a complete education from twelve to twenty-one, not needing a removal to any other place of learning. There is something strange in the idea of welding together the school and university, but it was more consonant to the opinions and practice of Milton's own age. He himself spent at the university the years between fourteen and twenty-one; the ordinary length of the academical course being seven years from entrance to the degree of M.A. So that his proposal is not so much to suppress the university as the school. Doubtless he saw little hope of reforming a large body like the university, or weaning it from the useless babblements of the Aristotelian philosophy, whereas by a private establishment such as he describes the reform might be begun at once. We must remember also that the age of entrance at public schools is now what the age of entrance at the university was in Milton's time; while many of our public school boys do not go to the university at all. The plan advocated by Milton is in this respect carried out in France, and pupils graduate directly from the *lycée*, only attending afterwards a special school of law or physic. Such institutions as Owens College at Manchester are doing precisely the work which Milton recommends.

Milton divides his scheme of education into three parts: (1) Studies; (2) Exercises; (3) Diet. In order to do justice to his method we must remember that he does not conceive of any education possible except through the Latin or Greek tongues. To make his precepts useful to us we must tear aside this veil, and go as deeply as we can into the principles which underlie his teaching, and infer what he would have recommended to us under a different state of things. In those days Latin was the language of the whole learned world. A man ignorant of Latin would have no access to the best books of the age, and no opportunity of communicating his thoughts to the world at large. It is natural, therefore, that he should recommend Latin grammar to be taught first, but with the Italian pronunciation of the vowels such as is rapidly making its way amongst us at the present day. But here at the outset the means are subordinate to the end. Language is to be the vehicle of moral teaching for the formation of a lofty character. The Pinax of Cebes, which as a school-book is coming now again into favour, and which advocates moral principles in simple language; the moral works of Plutarch, one of the purest and most high-minded of the ancients, and the best dialogues of Plato are to be read to the youthful scholars. For here Milton says, 'the main rule and ground-work will be to tempt them with such lectures and explanations upon every opportunity as may lead and draw them in willing obedience, enflamed with the study of learning and the admiration of virtue, cheered up with high hope of living to be brave men and worthy patriots, dear to God and famous to all ages.' Milton emphasises the cardinal truth of education, that it resides not in the mechanical perfection of study and routine, but in the spirit of the teacher working in the heart of the pupil. The first step in education is to make the pupils ' despise and scorn all their childish and ill-taught qualities, to delight in manly and liberal exercises, to infuse into their young hearts such an ingenuous and noble ardour as would not fail to make many of them renowned and matchless men.' Together with their Latin exercises, arithmetic, and geometry, are to be taught playing, 'as the old manner was,' and religion is to occupy them before going to bed. Thus ends the first stage of their education. It should be remarked that the Greek authors, Cebes, Plutarch, and Plato, are to be read, of course in Latin translations, and that they are to be 'read to' the boys probably in the manner recommended by Ratich and Ascham. As soon as they are masters of the rudiments of Latin Grammar they are to read those treatises, such as Cato, Varro, and Columella, which are concerned with agriculture. The object of this is not only to teach them Latin but to incite and enable them to improve the tillage of their country, to remove the bad soil and to remedy the waste that is made of good. Then after learning the use of globes and maps, and the outlines of geography, ancient and modern, they are to read some compendious method of natural philosophy. After this they are to begin Greek, but the authors read have reference to natural science, which is at this period the staple of their education. When in their mathematical studies they have reached trigonometry, that will introduce them to fortification, architecture, engineering, and navigation. They are to proceed in the study of nature as far as anatomy, and they are to acquire the principles of medicine that they may know the tempers, the humours, the seasons, and how to manage a crudity. No advocate of scientific education could have sketched out a more comprehensive plan of study in these departments.

Then follows a suggestion which has often been made by educational theorists, but not often tried. There are some minds which are inaccessible to purely abstract knowledge ; learning takes no hold on them unless it is connected with doing, and it has occurred to many that, if to the whole curriculum of science there could be added a curriculum of practice, few pupils would be found incapable of receiving intellectual education. We find this feature in the Pædagogic Province of Goethe's 'Wilhelm Meister,' and the few occasions on which it has been tried give encouragement for its further use. Milton accepts it without reserve. 'To set forward all these proceedings in nature and mathematics, what hinders but they may procure, as oft as shall be needful, the helpful experiences of hunters, fowlers, fishermen, shepherds, gardeners, apothecaries, and, in the other sciences, architects, engineers, anatomists, who, doubtless, would be ready, some for reward and some to favour such a hopeful seminary. And this will give them such a real tincture of natural knowledge as they will never forget, but daily augment with delight.'

These rudimentary studies, classical, mathematical, and practical, may be supposed to have occupied them to the age of sixteen, when they are for the first time to be introduced to graver and harder topics. 'As they begin to acquire character, and to reason on the difference between good and evil, there will be required a constant and sound indoctrinating to set them right and firm, instructing them more amply in the knowledge of virtue and the hatred of vice. For this purpose their young and pliant affections are to be led through the moral works of Plato, Xenophon, Cicero, and Plutarch, but in their nightward studies they are to submit to the more determinate sentence of Holy Writ.' Thus they will have traversed the circle of ethical teaching. During this and the preceding stage, poetry is to be read as an amusement, and as a golden fringe to the practice of serious labour. 'And either now,' Milton remarks, 'or before this, they may have easily learnt, at any odd hour, the Italian tongue.' This sentence has often been quoted to shew how visionary and baseless Milton's idea of education was. But experience is here in his favour, and those who have tried the experiment are well aware that Italian may easily be learnt by intelligent and studious boys with little expenditure of time or interruption of other studies. Ethics is to be succeeded by politics. After the foundation of their character and principles, then is to follow their education as citizens. They are to learn 'the beginning, end, and reason of political societies; that

they may not in a dangerous fit of the Common-
wealth be such poor, shaken, uncertain reeds, of
such a tottering conscience as many of our good
councillors have of late shewed themselves, but
steadfast pillars of the State.' The study of law is
to come next, including all the Roman edicts, and
tables with Justinian, and also the Saxon law, and
common law of England, and the statutes of the
realm. 'Sundays also and every evening may be
now understandingly spent in the highest matters
of theology, and Church history, ancient and modern.' By the age of eighteen Hebrew will have
been learnt, and possibly Syrian and Chaldaic.
Tragedy will be read and learned in close con-
nection with political oratory. 'These, if got by
memory and solemnly pronounced with right accent and grace, as might be taught, would endue
them even with the spirit and vigour of Demos-
thenes or Cicero, Euripides or Sophocles.' When
their minds are truly stored with this wealth of
learning, they are at length to acquire the art of
expression, both in writing and in speech. 'From
henceforth, and not till now, will be the right
season for forming them to be able writers and
composers in every excellent matter, when they
shall be thus fraught with an universal insight into
things.' Thus ends this magnificent and comprehensive scheme. 'These are the studies wherein
our noble and our gentle youth' (observe that
Milton is thinking of the education of a gentleman)
'ought to bestow their time in a disciplinary way

from twelve to one-and-twenty, unless they rely more upon their ancestors dead than upon themselves living.   In the which methodical course it is so supposed they must proceed by the steady pace of learning onward, as in convenient times to retire back into the middle ward, and sometimes into the rear of what they have been taught, until they have confirmed and solidly united the whole body of their perfected knowledge like the last embattelling of a Roman legion.'

One of the main hopes of the improvement of education lies in adopting the truth that manly and serious studies are capable of being handled and mastered by intelligent schoolboys. We might have hoped that the publication of John Stuart Mill's 'Autobiography' would have led to the imitation of the method by which he gained a start of twenty years over his contemporaries in the race of life.   It seems to have produced the contrary effect.   But no one can read Mill's letters to Sir S. Bentham without acknowledging that he had done at the age of thirteen nearly as much as Milton expected from his matured students.   Mill was reading Thucydides, Euclid, and algebra at eight, Pindar and conic sections at nine, trigonometry at ten, Aristotle at eleven, optics and fluxions at twelve, logic and political economy at thirteen. He had also by this time written two histories and a tragedy.   There is no reason to suppose that the studies thus early acquired did not form an integral part of his mind, or that when writing his

standard works on logic and political economy, or
sketching a complete scheme of education at St
Andrew's, he was not using the knowledge which
he had acquired in these very tender years.

The physical exercise proposed by Milton for
his students is of an equally practical character,
and differs widely from the laborious toiling at
unproductive games, which is the practice of our
own day. With him amusement, emulation, bodily
skill, the cheerfulness of bright companionship, are
all pressed into the service of practical life. Dinner
is taken at noon, and about an hour or an hour
and a half before that meal is to be allowed them
for exercise, and rest afterwards. The first exercise recommended is 'the use of the sword, to
guard and to strike safely with edge or point.
This will keep them healthy, nimble, strong, and
well in breath, is also the likeliest means to make
them grow large and tall, and to inspire them with
a gallant and fearless courage.' They are also to
be practised in 'all the locks and gripes of wrestling.' After about an hour of such exercise, during
the needful repose which precedes their mid-day
meal, they may 'with profit and delight be taken
up in recruiting and composing their travailed
spirits with the solemn and divine harmonies of
music, heard or learnt, either while the skilful organist plies his grave and fancied descant in lofty
fugues, or the whole symphony with artful and
unimaginable touches adorn and grace the well-
studied chords of some choice composer. Some-

times the lute or soft organ-stop, waiting on elegant
voices either to religious, martial, or civil ditties,
which, if wise men and prophets be not extremely
out, have a great power over dispositions and manners, to smooth and make them gentle from rustic
harshness and distempered passions.' The same
rest, with the same accompaniment, is to follow
after food. About two hours before supper, which
I suppose would be at about seven or eight o'clock,
'they are by a sudden alarum or watchword to
be called out to their military motions under sky
or covert, according to the season, as was the Roman wont, first on foot, then, as their age permits,
on horseback, to all the arts of cavalry ; that having in sport, but with much exertion and daily
muster, served out the rudiments of their soldier-
ship in all the skill of encamping, marching, embattelling, fortifying, besieging and battering, with
all the help of ancient and modern stratagems,
tactics, and warlike maxims, they may, as it were,
out of a long war come forth renowned and perfect
commanders in the service of their country.' Milton had good reason' to desire the formation of
the nucleus of a citizen army, and much service
might be rendered by a school rifle corps if they
were organised on a more serious and laborious
model.

In Milton's institution the vacations were intended to be short, but the time was not all to be
spent in work without a break. ' In those vernal
seasons of the year, when the air is calm and

pleasant, it were an injury and sullenness against nature not to go out and see her riches, and partake in her rejoicing with heaven and earth. I should not therefore be a persuader to them of studying much then, after two or three years, that they have well laid their grounds, but to ride out in companies with prudent and staid guides into all quarters of the land, learning and observing all places of strength, all commodities of building and of soil for towns and villages, harbours and ports of trade; sometimes taking sea as far as our navy, to learn also what they can in the practical knowledge of sailing and sea fights. These journeys would try all their peculiarities of nature, and if there were any such excellence among them would fetch it out, and give it fair opportunities to advance itself by.' 'This,' he says, 'will be much better than asking Monsieur of Paris to take our hopeful youths into their slight and prodigal custody, and send them back transformed into mimics, apes and kickshoes.' Travelling abroad is to be deferred to the age of three-and-twenty, when they will be better able to profit by it. In Milton's time communication was far more difficult than it is now. Not only was a short trip on the Continent out of the question, but even travelling in England was laborious and slow. Yet even in these days our young statesmen are profoundly ignorant of the country to which they belong, and a knowledge of its character and resources should be the first foundation of sound political wisdom.

In our own day we might go so far as to regard a knowledge of the whole world as the fitting conclusion to a liberal education, and Milton, if he were writing now, might recommend an educational cruise such as has been attempted in America and France. Of diet, his last division, Milton tells us nothing except that it should be in the same house, and that it should be plain, healthful, and moderate.

In conclusion Milton anticipates some of the objections which might be raised against his plan, on the score of its impracticability, or its aiming at too high a standard. He admits that a scheme of this kind cannot be carried out except under the most favourable conditions, with teachers and scholars above the average. 'I believe,' he says, 'that this is not a bow for every man to shoot in, that counts himself a teacher; but will require sinews almost equal to those which Homer gave Ulysses; yet I am withal persuaded that it may prove much more easy in the essay than it now seems at a distance, and much more illustrious, howbeit, not more difficult than I imagine, and that imagination presents me with nothing else, but very happy and very possible, according to best wishes, if God have so decreed, and this age have spirit and capacity enough to apprehend.'

OF

EDUCATION.

To Master *Samuel Hartlib.*

Written above twenty Years since.

Mr. *Hartlib,*

I Am long since perswaded, that to say, or do ought worth memory and imitation, no purpose or respect should sooner move us, then simply the love of God, and of mankind. Nevertheless to write now the reforming of Education, though it be one of the greatest and noblest designs that can be thought on, and for the want whereof this Nation perishes, I had not yet at this time been induc't, but by your earnest entreaties, and serious conjurements ; as having my mind for the present half diverted in the pursuance of some other assertions, the knowledge and the use of which, cannot but be a great furtherance both to the enlargement of truth, and

honest

honest living, with much more peace. Nor should the laws of any private friendship have prevail'd with me to divide thus, or transpose my former thoughts, but that I see those aims, those actions which have won you with me the esteem of a person sent hither by some good providence from a far country to be the occasion and the incitement of great good to this Island. And, as I hear, you have obtain'd the same repute with men of most approved wisdom, and some of highest authority among us. Not to mention the learned correspondence which you hold in forreign parts, and the extraordinary pains and diligence which you have us'd in this matter both here, and beyond the Seas; either by the definite will of God so ruling, or the peculiar sway of nature, which also is Gods working. Neither can I think that so reputed, and so valu'd as you are, you would to the forfeit of your own discerning ability, impose upon me an unfit and over-ponderous argument, but that the satisfaction which you profess to have receiv'd from those incidental Discourses which we have wander'd into, hath prest and almost constrain'd you into a perswasion, that what you require from me in this point, I neither ought, nor can in conscience deferre beyond this time both of so much need

at

at once, and so much opportunity to try what God hath determin'd. I will not resist therefore, whatever it is either of divine, or humane obligement that you lay upon me; but will forthwith set down in writing, as you request me, that voluntary *Idea*, which hath long in silence presented it self to me, of a better Education, in extent and comprehension far more large, and yet of time far shorter, and of attainment far more certain, then hath been yet in practice. Brief I shall endeavour to be; for that which I have to say, assuredly this Nation hath extream need should be done sooner then spoken. To tell you therefore what I have benefited herein among old renowned Authors, I shall spare; and to search what many modern *Janua's* and *Didactics* more then ever I shall read, have projected, my inclination leads me not. But if you can accept of these few observations which have flowr'd off, and are, as it were, the burnishing of many studious and contemplative years altogether spent in the search of religious and civil knowledge, and such as pleas'd you so well in the relating, I here give you them to dispose of.

The end then of Learning is to repair the ruines of our first Parents by regaining to know God aright, and out of that knowledge to love

him,

him, to imitate him, to be like him, as we may the neerest by possessing our souls of true vertue, which being united to the heavenly grace of faith makes up the highest perfection. But because our understanding cannot in this body found it self but on sensible things, nor arrive so clearly to the knowledge of God and things invisible, as by orderly conning over the visible and inferior creature, the same method is necessarily to be follow'd in all discreet teaching. And seeing every Nation affords not experience and tradition enough for all kind of Learning, therefore we are chiefly taught the Languages of those people who have at any time been most industrious after Wisdom ; so that Language is but the Instrument conveying to us things usefull to be known. And though a Linguist should pride himself to have all the Tongues that *Babel* cleft the world into, yet, if he have not studied the solid things in them as well as the Words & Lexicons, he were nothing so much to be esteem'd a learned man, as any Yeoman or Tradesman competently wise in his Mother Dialect only. Hence appear the many mistakes which have made Learning generally so unpleasing and so unsuccessful; first we do amiss to spend seven or eight years meerly in scraping together so
much

much miserable Latine and Greek, as might be learnt otherwise easily and delightfully in one year. And that which casts our proficiency therein so much behind, is our time lost partly in too oft idle vacancies given both to Schools and Universities, partly in a preposterous exaction, forcing the empty wits of Children to compose Theams, Verses and Orations, which are the acts of ripest judgment and the final work of a head fill'd by long reading and observing, with elegant maxims, and copious invention. These are not matters to be wrung from poor striplings, like blood out of the Nose, or the plucking of untimely fruit : besides the ill habit which they get of wretched barbarizing against the Latin and Greek *idiom*, with their untutor'd *Anglicisms*, odious to be read, yet not to be avoided without a well continu'd and judicious conversing among pure Authors digested, which they scarce taste, whereas, if after some preparatory grounds of speech by their certain forms got into memory, they were led to the praxis thereof in some chosen short book lesson'd throughly to them, they might then forthwith proceed to learn the substance of good things, and Arts in due order, which would bring the whole language quickly into their power. This I take to be the most rational

and

and most profitable way of learning Languages,
and whereby we may best hope to give account
to God of our youth spent herein: And for the
usual method of teaching Arts, I deem it to be
an old errour of Universities not yet well recover'd from the Scholastick grossness of bar-
barous ages, that in stead of beginning with
Arts most easie, and those be such as are most
obvious to the sence, they present their young
unmatriculated Novices at first comming with
the most intellective abstractions of Logick and
Metaphysicks ; So that they having but newly
left those Grammatick flats and shallows where
they stuck unreasonably to learn a few words
with lamentable construction, and now on the
sudden transported under another climate to
be tost and turmoil'd with their unballasted
wits in fadomless and unquiet deeps of controversie, do for the most part grow into hatred
and contempt of Learning, mockt and delu-
ded all this while with ragged Notions and
Babblements, while they expected worthy
and delightful knowledge ; till poverty or
youthful years call them importunately their
several wayes, and hasten them with the sway
of friends either to an ambitious and mercenary, or ignorantly zealous Divinity ; Some
allur'd to the trade of Law, grounding their

purposes

purposes not on the prudent and heavenly contemplation of justice and equity which was never taught them, but on the promising and pleasing thoughts of litigious terms, fat contentions. and flowing fees ; others betake them to State affairs, with souls so unprincipl'd in vertue, and true generous breeding, that flattery, and Court shifts and tyrannous Aphorisms appear to them the highest points of wisdom ; instilling their barren hearts with a conscientious slavery, if, as I rather think, it be not fain'd. Others lastly of a more delicious and airie spirit, retire themselves knowing no better, to the enjoyments of ease and luxury, living out their daies in feast and jollity ; which indeed is the wisest and the safest course of all these, unless they were with more integrity undertaken. And these are the fruits of mispending our prime youth at the Schools and Universities as we do, either in learning meer words or such things chiefly, as were better unlearnt.

I shall detain you no longer in the demonstration of what we should not do, but strait conduct ye to a hill side, where I will point ye out the right path of a vertuous and noble Education; laborious indeed at the first ascent, but else so smooth, so green, so full of goodly

prospect,

prospect, and melodious sounds on every side, that the Harp of *Orpheus* was not more charming. I doubt not but ye shall have more adoe to drive our dullest and laziest youth, our stocks and stubbs from the infinite desire of such a happy nurture, then we have now to hale and drag our choicest and hopefullest Wits to that asinine feast of sowthistles and brambles which is commonly set before them, as all the food and entertainment of their tenderest and most docible age. I call therefore a compleat and generous Education that which fits a man to perform justly, skilfully and magnanimously all the offices both private and publick of Peace and War. And how all this may be done between twelve, and one and twenty, less time then is now bestow'd in pure trifling at Grammar and *Sophistry*, is to be thus order'd.

First to find out a spatious house and ground about it fit for an *Academy*, and big enough to lodge a hundred and fifty persons, whereof twenty or thereabout may be attendants, all under the government of one, who shall be thought of desert sufficient, and ability either to do all, or wisely to direct, and oversee it done. This place should be at once both School and University, not heeding a remove to any other house of Schollership, except it be be some peculiar Colledge of Law, or Physick, where they mean to be practitioners ; but as for those general studies which take up all our time from *Lilly* to the commencing, as they term it, Master of Art, it should be absolute. After this pattern, as many Edifices may be converted to this use, as shall be needful in every City throughout this Land, which would tend much to the encrease of Learning and Civility every where. This number, less or more thus collected, to the convenience of a foot Company, or interchangeably two Troops of Cavalry, should divide their daies work into three parts, as it lies orderly. Their Stu - dies, their Exercise, and their Diet.

For their Studies, First they should begin with the chief and necessary rules of some good Grammar, either that now us'd, or any better : and while this is doing, their speech is to be fashion'd to a distinct and clear pro- nuntiation, as near as may be to the *Italian*, especially in the Vowels. For we *Englishmen* being far Northerly, do not open our mouths in the cold air, wide enough to grace a Southern Tongue ; but are observ'd by all other Nations to speak exceeding close and inward : So that to smatter Latine with an English mouth, is as ill a hearing as Law-
French.

French. Next to make them expert in the usefullest points of Grammar, and withall to season them, and win them early to the love of vertue and true labour, ere any flattering seducement, or vain principle seise them wandering, some easie and delightful Book of Education would be read to them ; whereof the Greeks have store, as *Cebes*, *Plutarch*, and other Socratic discourses. But in Latin we have none of classic authority extant, except the two or three first Books of *Quintilian*, and some select pieces elsewhere. But here the main skill and groundwork will be, to temper them such Lectures and Explanations upon every opportunity, as may lead and draw them in willing obedience, enflam'd with the study of Learning, and the admiration of Vertue ; stirr'd up with high hopes of living to be brave men, and worthy Patriots, dear to God, and famous to all ages. That they may despise and scorn all their childish, and ill-taught qualities, to delight in manly, and liberal Exercises : which he who hath the Art, and proper Eloquence to catch them with, what with mild and effectual perswasions, and what with the intimation of some fear, if need be, but chiefly by his own example, might in a short space gain them to an incredible diligence and courage

rage : infusing into their young brests such an ingenuous and noble ardor, as would not fail to make many of them renowned and match-less men. At the same time, some other hour of the day, might be taught them the rules of Arithmetick, and soon after the Elements of Geometry even playing, as the old manner was. After evening repast, till bed-time their thoughts will be best taken up in the easie grounds of Religion, and the story of Scrip-ture. The next step would be to the Authors *Agriculture, Cato, Varro,* and *Columella,* for the matter is most easie, and if the language be difficult, so much the better, it is not a difficulty above their years. And here will be an occasion of inciting and inabling them here-after to improve the tillage of their Country, to recover the bad Soil, and to remedy the waste that is made of good: for this was one of *Hercules* praises. Ere half these Authors be read (which will soon be with plying hard, and daily) they cannot chuse but be masters of any ordinary prose. So that it will be then seasonable for them to learn in any modern Author, the use of the Globes, and all the Maps ; first with the old names, and then with the new : or they might be then capable to read any compendious method of natural Phi-losophy.

losophy. And at the same time might be entering into the Greek tongue, after the same manner as was before prescrib'd in the Latin; whereby the difficulties of Grammar being soon overcome, all the Historical Physiology of *Aristotle* and *Theophrastus* are open before them, and as I may say, under contribution. The like access will be to *Vitruvius*, to *Seneca's* natural questions, to *Mela, Celsus, Pliny*, or *Solinus*. And having thus past the principles of *Arithmetick, Geometry, Astronomy*, and *Geography* with a general compact of Physicks, they may descend in *Mathematicks* to the instrumental science of *Trigonometry*, and from thence to Fortification, Architecture, Enginry, or Navigation. And in natural Philosophy they may proceed leisurely from the History of Meteors, Minerals, plants and living Creatures as far as Anatomy. Then also in course might be read to them out of some not tedious Writer the Institution of Physick; that they may know the tempers, the humours, the seasons, and how to manage a crudity: which he who can wisely and timely do, is not only a great Physitian to himself, and to his friends, but also may at some time or other, save an Army by this frugal and expenseless means only; and not let the healthy and stout bodies of young men rot

away

away under him for want of this discipline; which is a great pity, and no less a shame to the Commander. To set forward all these proceedings in Nature and Mathematicks, what hinders, but that they may procure, as oft as shal be needful, the helpful experiences of Hunters, Fowlers, Fishermen, Shepherds, Gardeners, Apothecaries; and in the other sciences, Architects, Engineers, Mariners, Anatomists; who doubtless would be ready some for reward, and some to favour such a hopeful Seminary. And this will give them such a real tincture of natural knowledge, as they shall never forget, but daily augment with delight. Then also those Poets which are now counted most hard, will be both facil and pleasant, *Orpheus, Hesiod, Theocritus, Aratus, Nicander, Oppian, Dionysius,* and in Latin *Lucretius, Manilius,* and the rural part of *Virgil.*

By this time, years and good general precepts will have furnisht them more distinctly with that act of reason which in *Ethicks* is call'd *Proairesis:* that they may with some judgement contemplate upon moral good and evil. Then will be requir'd a special reinforcement of constant and sound endoctrinating to set them right and firm, instructing them more amply in the knowledge of Vertue and the hatred of Vice:

Vice : while their young and pliant affections are led through all the moral works of
Plato, Xenophon, Cicero, Plutarch, Laertius, and
those *Locrian* remnants; but still to be reduc't
in their nightward studies wherewith they
close the dayes work, under the determinate
sentence of *David* or *Salomon,* or the Evanges
and Apostolic Scriptures. Being perfect in the
knowledge of personal duty, they may then
begin the study of Economics. And either
now, or before this, they may have easily learnt
at any odd hour the *Italian Tongue.* And
soon after, but with wariness and good antidote, it would be wholesome enough to let
them taste some choice Comedies, Greek, Latin,
or *Italian :* Those Tragedies also that treat of
Household matters, as *Trachiniæ, Alcestis,* and
the like. The next remove must be to the
study of *Politicks ;* to know the beginning,
end, and reasons of Political Societies ; that
they may not in a dangerous fit of the Common-wealth be such poor, shaken, uncertain
Reeds, of such a tottering Conscience, as many
of our great Counsellers have lately shewn
themselves, but stedfast pillars of the State.
After this they are to dive into the grounds of
Law, and legal Justice ; deliver'd first, and
with best warrant by *Moses ;* and as far as humane

mane prudence can be trusted, in those ex-
toll'd remains of Grecian Law-givers, *Licurgus,
Solon, Zaleucus, Charondas,* and thence to all the
Roman *Edicts* and Tables with their *Justinian;*
and so down to the *Saxon* and common Laws
of *England,* and the Statutes. Sundayes also and
every evening may be now understandingly
spent in the highest matters of *Theology,* and
Church History ancient and modern : and ere
this time the Hebrew Tongue at a set hour
might have been gain'd, that the Scriptures
may be now read in their own orginal ; where-
to it would be no impossibility to add the
Chaldey, and the *Syrian* Dialect. When all
these employments are well conquer'd, then
will the choice Histories, *Heroic Poems,* and
Attic Tragedies of stateliest and most regal argument, with all the famous Political Orations offer themselves ; which if they were not
only read ; but some of them got by memory,
and solemnly pronounc't with right accent,
and grace, as might be taught, would endue
them even with the spirit and vigor of *De-
mosthenes* or *Cicero, Euripides,* or *Sophocles.*
And now lastly will be the time to read with
them those organic arts which inable men to
discourse and write perspicuously, elegantly,
and according to the fitted stile of lofty, mean,

or

or lowly. Logic therefore so much as is useful, is to be referr'd to this due place withall her well coucht Heads and Topics, untill it be time to open her contracted palm into a gracefull and ornate Rhetorick taught out of the rule of *Plato, Aristotle, Phalereus, Cicero, Hermogenes, Longinus.* To which Poetry would be made subsequent, or indeed rather precedent, as being less suttle and fine, but more simple, sensuous and passionate. I mean not here the prosody of a verse, which they could not but have hit on before among the rudiments of Grammar; but that sublime Art which in *Aristotles Poetics*, in *Horace*, and the *Italian* Commentaries of *Castelvetro, Tasso, Mazzoni,* and others, teaches what the laws are of a true *Epic* Poem, what of a *Dramatic*, what of a *Lyric*, what Decorum is, which is the grand master-piece to observe. This would make them soon perceive what despicable creatures our comm Rimers and Play-writers be, and shew them, what religious, what glorious and magnificent use might be made of Poetry both in divine and humane things. From hence and not till now will be the right season of forming them to be able Writers and Composers in every excellent matter, when they shall be thus fraught with an universal insight into things.

things. Or whether they be to speak in Parliament or Counsel, honour and attention would be waiting on their lips. There would then also appear in Pulpits other Visages, other gestures, and stuff otherwise wrought then what we now sit under, oft times to as great a trial of our patience as any other that they preach to us. These are the Studies wherein our noble and our gentle Youth ought to bestow their time in a disciplinary way from twelve to one and twenty ; unless they rely more upon their ancestors dead, then upon themselves living. In which methodical course it is so suppos'd they must proceed by the steddy pace of learning onward, as at convenient times for memories sake to retire back into the middle ward, and sometimes into the rear of what they have been taught, untill they have confirm'd, and solidly united the whole body of their perfeted knowledge, like the last embattelling of a Roman Legion. Now will be worth the seeing what Exercises and Recreations may best agree, and become these Studies.

Their Exercise.

The course of Study hitherto briefly describ'd, is, what I can guess by reading, likest

to

to those ancient and famous Schools of *Pytha-goras, Plato, Isocrates, Aristotle* and such others, out of which were bred up such a number of renowned Philosophers, Orators, Historians, Poets and Princes all over *Greece, Italy,* and *Asia,* besides the flourishing Studies of *Cyrene* and *Alexandria.* But herein it shall exceed them, and supply a defect as great as that which *Plato* noted in the Common-wealth of *Sparta;* whereas that City train'd up their Youth most for War, and these in their Academies and *Lycæum,* all for the Gown, this institution of breeding which I here delineate, shall be equally good both for Peace and War. Therefore about an hour and a half ere they eat at Noon should be allow'd them for exercise and due rest afterwards: But the time for this may be enlarg'd at pleasure, according as their rising in the morning shall be early. The Exercise which I commend first, is the exact use of their Weapon, to guard and to strike safely with edge, or point; this will keep them healthy, nimble, strong, and well in breath, is also the likeliest means to make them grow large and tall, and to inspire them with a gallant and fearless courage, which being temper'd with seasonable Lectures and Precepts to them of true Fortitude and Patience, will turn into a

native

native and heroick valour, and make them hate the cowardise of doing wrong. They must be also practiz'd in all the Locks and Gripes of Wrastling, wherein English men were wont to excell, as need may often be in fight to tugg or grapple, and to close. And this perhaps will be enough, wherein to prove and heat their single strength. The interim of unsweating themselves regularly, and convevenient rest before meat may both with profit and delight be taken up in recreating and composing their travail'd spirits with the solemn and divine harmonies of Musick heard or learnt; either while the skilful *Organist* plies his grave and fancied descant, in lofty fugues, or the whole Symphony with artful and unimaginable touches adorn and grace the well studied chords of some choice Composer, sometimes the Lute, or soft Organ stop waiting on elegant Voices either to Religious, martial, or civil Ditties ; which if wise men and Prophets be not extreamly out, have a great power over dispositions and manners, to smooth and make them gentle from rustick harshness and distemper'd passions. The like also would not be unexpedient after Meat to assist and cherish Nature in her first concoction, and send their minds back to study in good
tune

tune and satisfaction. Where having follow'd it close under vigilant eyes till about two hours before supper, they are by a sudden alarum or watch word, to be call'd out to their military motions, under skie or covert, according to the season, as was the Roman wont : first on foot, then as their age permits, on Horseback, to all the Art of Cavalry ; That having in sport, but with much exactness, and daily muster, serv'd out the rudiments of their Souldiership in all the skill of Embattelling, Marching, Encamping, Fortifying, Besieging and Battering, with all the helps of ancient and modern stratagems, *Tacticks* and warlike maxims, they may as it were out of a long War come forth renowned and perfect Commanders in the service of their Country. They would not then, if they were trusted with fair and hopeful armies, suffer them for want of just and wise discipline to shed away from about them like sick feathers, though they be never so oft suppli'd : they would not suffer their empty and unrecrutible Colonels of twenty men in a Company to quaff out, or convey into secret hoards, the wages of a delusive list, and a miserable remnant : yet in the mean while to be over-master'd with a score or two of drunkards, the only souldery left about them, or

else

else to comply with all rapines and violences. No certainly, if they knew ought of that knowledge that belongs to good men or good Governours, they would not suffer these things. But to return to our own institute, besides these constant exercises at home, there is another opportunity of gaining experience to be won from pleasure it self abroad; In those vernal seasons of the year, when the air is calm and pleasant, it were an injury and sullenness against nature not to go out, and see her riches, and partake in her rejoycing with Heaven and Earth. I should not therefore be a perswader to them of studying much then, after two or three year that they have well laid their grounds, but to ride out in Companies with prudent and staid Guides, to all the quarters of the Land: learning and observing all places of strength, all commodities of building and of soil, for Towns and Tillage, Harbours and Ports for Trade. Sometimes taking Sea as far as to our Navy, to learn there also what they can in the practical knowledge of sailing and of Sea-fight. These ways would try all their peculiar gifts of Nature, and if there were any secret excellence among them, would fetch it out, and give it fair opportunities to advance it self by, which could

not

not but mightily redound to the good of this
Nation, and bring into fashion again those
old admired Vertues and Excellencies, with
far more advantage now in this purity of Chri-
stian knowledge. Nor shall we then need
the *Monsieurs* of *Paris* to take our hopefull
Youth into their slight and prodigal custodies
and send them over back again transform'd
into Mimicks, Apes and Kicshoes. But if
they desire to see other Countries at three or
four and twenty years of age, not to learn
Principles but to enlarge Experience, and
make wise observation, they will by that time
be such as shall deserve the regard and honour
of all men where they pass, and the society
and friendship of those in all places who are
best and most eminent. And perhaps then
other Nations will be glad to visit us for their
Breeding, or else to imitate us in their own
Country.

Now lastly for their Diet there cannot be
much to say, save only that it would be best
in the same House ; for much time else would
be lost abroad, and many ill habits got ; and
that it should be plain, healthful, and moderate I suppose is out of controversie. Thus
Mr. *Hartlib*, you have a general view in writing, as your desire was, of that which at several

veral times I had discourst with you concerning the best and Noblest way of Education;
not beginning as some have done from the
Cradle, which yet might be worth many con-
siderations, if brevity had not been my scope,
many other circumstances also I could have
mention'd, but this to such as have the worth
in them to make trial, for light and direction
may be enough. Only I believe that this is
not a Bow for every man to shoot in that
counts himself a Teacher; but will require
sinews almost equal to those which *Homer* gave
Ulysses, yet I am withall perswaded that it may
prove much more easie in the assay, then it
now seems at distance, and much more illustrious: howbeit not more difficult then I
imagine, and that imagination presents me with
nothing but very happy and very possible according to best wishes; if God have so decreed, and this age have spirit and capacity
enough to apprehend.

NOTES.

To Master Samuel Hartlib. For an account of
Samuel Hartlib see Masson's *Life of Milton*, III. 193.
He was the son of a Polish merchant of German extrac-
tion, who had settled at Elbing in Prussia. His mother
was the daughter of an English merchant at Danzic, so
Hartlib though Prussian born with Polish connexions
could call himself half English. He was probably about
eight or ten years older than Milton. He first came to
England about the year 1628 and from that time made
London his headquarters. "He was one of those
persons now styled 'philanthropists' or 'friends of
progress,' who take an interest in every question or
project of their time promising social improvement, have
always some iron in the fire, are constantly forming
committees or writing letters to persons of influence and
altogether live for the public. By the common consent
of all who have explored the intellectual and social
history of England in the seventeenth century, he is one
of the most interesting and memorable figures of that
whole period."

written above twenty years since. According to Masson,
Life of Milton, III. 233. The treatise "of Education"

4—2

was first published on June 5, 1644. The treatise was reprinted in 1673 at the end of the second edition of the minor poems with the words "written above twenty years since" (really nearly thirty) added to the original title. The text of the present edition is a fac-simile of the reprint of 1673.

l. 8. *respect*, consideration.

l. 9. *then.* The old spelling of than, as our then was then spelt than, and in Shakespere's *Lucrece* rhymes to van and began.

l. 17. *conjurements*, "solemn appeals."

l. 18. *diverted*, "turned off."

l. 19. *assertions*, positions, statements. Milton's mind was now principally occupied with the questions of Divorce and of the liberty of unlicensed printing. The second edition of the *Doctrine and Discipline of Divorce* was published about three months before the *Tractate*, and his *Judgement of Master Bucer concerning Divorce* five weeks after. The *Areopagitica* was published Nov. 24, 1644.

P. 2, l. 3. *divide*, to break up. *transpose*, to change.

l. 6. *person sent hither*, John Amos Comenius. For an account of him see *John Amos Comenius* by S. S. Laurie in Kegan Paul's *Education Library*, also Masson's *Life of Milton*, vol. III. There are also accounts of him in Browning's *History of Educational Theories*, and Quick's *Educational Reformers.* Comenius came to London at Hartlib's invitation, Sept. 22, 1641. He left it for Sweden in August, 1642. When he was in London the Parliament thought of assigning to Comenius for his plans of a College-University some College with its revenues. Comenius tells us "there was even named for the purpose the *Savoy* in London; *Winchester College* out of London was named; and again nearer the city *Chelsea College,* inventories of which and of its revenues were communicated to us; so that nothing seemed more certain than that the design of the great Verulam concerning the opening somewhere of a Universal College devoted to the advancement of the Sciences, would be carried out. But the rumour of the insurrection in Ireland and of the massacre in one night of more than 200,000 English, and the sudden departure of the King from London, and the plentiful signs of the bloody war about to break out disturbed these plans, and obliged me to hasten my return to my own people."

l. 15. *beyond the seas.* Comenius spent the years 1643—1646 at Elbing, Hartlib's own birthplace, writing his didactic treatises, and his going there was largely owing to Hartlib's recommendation.

P. 3, l. 4. *obligement,* duty, obligation.

l. 17. *Janua's and Didactics.* This is a reference apparently a little contemptuous to Comenius's two great works; the *Janua linguarum reserata* was published in 1631, and was translated into most European and some Eastern languages. His *Didactica Magna* was first written in his own language, Czech, and afterwards translated into Latin. It is doubtful if it was published in 1644, but Milton had of course heard of it.

l. 20. *flowr'd off.* Latham explains this as "come off as flowers by sublimation." I should rather connect it with the "burnishing" below.

l. 21. *burnishing,* the particles rubbed off in polishing.

l. 27. *ruines,* the fall.

P. 4, l. 6. *sensible things.* This is the keynote of Milton's teaching. *Things* are to be taught before *words,* or rather *things* and *words* are to be taught together, the only value of *words* being that they lead us to the *things* of which they are symbols, as he says below "language is but the *instrument* conveying to us *things* usefull to be known."

P. 5, l. 5. *idle vacancies.* This probably does not refer so much to vacations and holidays as to perpetual interruption caused by Saints' days and holidays. This is a principal cause of the inefficiency of the education given by Jesuits and other Roman Catholic bodies. At Eton College, when I was a boy there, every Saint's day was a holiday and every eve a half-holiday, the work of these days was supposed to be done on other days, so also at the University there were no lectures on Saints' days. The long vacation at the University of course existed in Milton's time.

l. 6. *preposterous*, inverting the natural order.

l. 15. *barbarizing*, so a lexicon of pure idiomatic latinity is called *antibarbarus.*

l. 16. *untutor'd*, rude, raw. So Shakespere *Lucrece*, Ded. "my untutored lines," and *II. Henry VI.* III. 2, "some stern untutored churl."

l. 19. *conversing among*, "becoming familiar with."

l. 21. *certain forms*, "paradigms," the regular forms in which they habitually occur.

l. 23. *lesson'd*, "taught."

l. 26. *Arts*, the subject-matter of a liberal education, originally the seven liberal arts contained in the Trivium and Quadrivium, Grammar, Dialectic, Rhetoric, Music, Arithmetic, Geometry, Astronomy. So Shakespere uses Arts as a synonym for education generally, *Taming of the Shrew*, I. 1. 2, "Padua, Nursery of Arts," and *Twelfth Night*, I. 3. 99, "Had I but followed the Arts." Compare Bachelor and Master of Arts.

P. 6, l. 9. *obvious to the sence.* This is an anticipation of the doctrines of Pestalozzi and Froebel, who insist on the importance of beginning education with the training of the senses.

l. 10. *unmatriculated,* "even before their matriculation," or perhaps generally "immature."

l. 11. *intellective,* "intellectual."

Logick. This is the same as Dialectic, and stands, as we have seen, second in the *Trivium,* immediately after Grammar. This is explained more in detail immediately below.

l. 18. *fadomless,* fathom is fadom in middle English.

l. 21. *ragged,* "rugged."

l. 22. *babblements,* "prattling."

l. 24. *youthful years,* the impatience of youth.

l. 25. *sway,* "pressure" or "influence."

l. 26. *mercenary...Divinity.* Such divines are treated with scathing scorn in *Lycidas,* where S. Peter says :

How well could I have spar'd for thee, young swain,
Anow of such as for their bellies' sake,
Creep and intrude, and climb into the fold?
Of other care they little reck'ning make,
Then how to scramble at the shearers' feast,
And shove away the worthy bidden guest ;
Blind mouthes ! that scarce themselves know how to hold
A sheep-hook, or have learn'd ought els the least
That to the faithfull Herdman's art belongs !
What recks it them ? What need they ? They are sped.

P. 7, l. 1. *prudent and heavenly contemplation. Prudent,* provident, foreseeing. Milton here sketches the idea of what a University law school ought to be, concerned with the theory and not with the practice of law.

l. 6. *State affairs.* Milton suggests the conception

of a University training for public and political life such as has never been found in England, but such as was contemplated by the creation of King's Scholars to be recommended for the service of the State, when the Regius Professorships of Modern History and Modern Languages were first founded by George I. at Oxford and Cambridge.

l. 11. *conscientious slavery.* They veil slavery under the form of conscientious subjection, but in this only deceive themselves.

l. 12. *delicious*, "delicate."

l. 13. *airie spirit*, a mind subject to spiritual influences.

l. 16. *wisest and the safest course*, compare *Lycidas:*

> "Were it not better done as others use
> To sport with Amaryllis in the shade
> Or with the tangles of Neæra's hair."

l. 19. *prime youth*, either our early youth or the best part of our youth.

l. 21. *meer words.* Milton returns here to the keynote of his argument, that the main fault of the present humanistic education is that it teaches *words* only.

P. 8, l. 2. *Harp of Orpheus.* Compare Shakespere, *Henry VIII*, Act III. sc. 1, "Orpheus with his lute made trees, And the mountain tops which freeze, Bow themselves when he did sing." Also *Merchant of Venice*, Act v. sc. 1, "therefore the poet Did feign that Orpheus drew trees, stones and floods, Since naught so stockish, hard and full of rage, But music for the time doth change his nature."

l. 5. *stocks and stubbs.* Stock is a log or post, the emblem of a senseless person. So *Taming of the Shrew,*

Act I. sc. 1, l. 31, "Let's be no stoics nor no stocks I pray." A stubb is the stock of a tree left when the rest is cut off. Spenser joins the two words together, "all about old stocks and stubbs of trees."

l. 7. *hale* = haul.

l. 11. *docible* = docile.

l. 18. *sophistry.* This would especially refer to Logic, the second of the seven *Arts*, following after Grammar.

P. 9, l. 2. *practitioners.* The school and university are to give the theoretical, not the practical and professional training; these in law and medicine are to be kept distinct.

l. 4. *Lilly*, as we should now say *the Latin Primer.* William Lilly (not to be confounded with John Lilly, the author of *Euphues*, who was born 30 years after this William Lilly's death) lived from about 1468 to 1523, and was an eminent scholar and first master of St Paul's School. He published in 1513, *Brevissima Institutio seu Ratio Grammatices cognoscendi*, generally known as *Lilly's Latin Grammar.* In this he was assisted by Colet, Cardinal Wolsey, and Erasmus.

commencing. The Great Commencement at Cambridge, the Comitia Magna, was the time at which the higher degrees were conferred.

l. 8. *every City.* It is important to notice that these Colleges were to be in towns, not in the country.

l. 10. *Civility*, what we should now call "culture."

l. 19. *their speech is to be fashion'd.* The first care in Greek education was to train the tender mouth and ear to express and distinguish between the delicate Greek vowels and the variety of accent. The teacher for this purpose was called the φώνασκος.

l. 27. *smatter.* Skeat says in his Dictionary, "*smat-*

ter (or *snatter*) is a frequentative verb from a base SMAK, SNAK denoting a smacking noise with the lips, hence a gabbling prating."

P. 10, l. 3. *season them*, imbue : so Jeremy Taylor, "secure their religion, *season* their younger years with prudent and pious principles."

l. 7. *read to them*. Mark this. In what language? Certainly not in Greek, perhaps not even in Latin. Masson says, "there were in Milton's time Latin translations of Cebes and at least one in English." Ratich, the forerunner of Comenius, advises the teacher of Latin to begin by translating the Latin author *to* the scholars first.

l. 8. *Cebes* was a disciple of Socrates, he is one of the speakers in the *Phædo* and was present at the death of Socrates. It is therefore rather remarkable that the πίναξ (pinax) of this author should have been so little studied in recent times. During the sixteenth and seventeenth centuries it was extremely popular. The genuineness of the treatise is, however, positively denied by Zeller who places it in a later age. The *Pinax* is a philosophical explanation of a table on which the whole of human life with its dangers and temptations were symbolically represented; "the author introduces some youths contemplating the table, and an old man who steps among them agrees to explain its meaning. The whole drift of the little book is to shew that only the proper development of our mind and the possession of real virtues can make us truly happy."

Plutarch flourished about A.D. 100. His moral works are here referred to which treat of education and domestic morality. They were translated into French by Amyot as early as 1565.

l. 9. *other Socratic discourses.* Milton of course believed the πίναξ of Cebes to be Socratic.

l. 11. *Quintilian,* for an account of his views on education see Browning's *Educational Theories,* p. 26. He was born A.D. 42 and was therefore a contemporary of Plutarch.

l. 13. *temper them,* to apportion or regulate for them, to suit the lessons to the occasion.

P. 11, l. 6. *arithmetick* and geometry were two of the seven liberal Arts coming in the Quadrivium after music and before astronomy.

l. 7. *playing, as the old manner was.* I have said elsewhere of Roman education (*Ed. Theor.* p. 21), "Next to reading and writing came reckoning, the fingers were made great use of, each joint and bend of the finger was made to signify a certain value, and the pupil was expected to follow the twinkling motion of the teacher's hands as he represented number after number. The modern Italian game of *mora* is a survival of this capacity." Plato more than once represents Socrates as giving lessons in geometry to young Greeks in the palæstra.

l. 9. *easie* = elementary.

l. 11. after *authors* 'of' should be inserted.

l. 12. *Cato* the censor (234—149 A.D.). The work *de Re Rustica* which bears his name is probably substantially his, but is not now in the form in which he left it. *Varro* wrote the three books *de Re Rustica* which we possess at the age of eighty, B.C. 36. He was an intimate friend of Cicero.

Columella who flourished a generation later wrote 12 books in agriculture. Milton mentions them in chronological order. The works of these three authors were first printed at Venice in 1472.

l. 14. *it is not a difficulty above their years.* Milton is quite right in assuming that children have little difficulty in learning a copious vocabulary. In these works the subject-matter and the construction are both of them easy.

l. 21. *plying,* "working steadily."

l. 22. *chuse but be,* "help being."

l. 23. *ordinary prose.* Latin prose is of course meant.

l. 24. *modern author,* probably in Latin.

P. 12, l. 5. *Historical* is probably used in the sense of "narrative." The title of Theophrastus' Greek work is ἡ περὶ φυτῶν ἱστορία.

l. 6. *Aristotle* lived 384—322 B.C. Theophrastus was his pupil; of his numerous works we only possess two on botany.

l. 8. *Vitruvius* lived in the time of Julius Cæsar and Augustus and wrote about architecture.

Seneca died A.D. 65, aged nearly 70. His *Questionum Naturalium libri septem* "is one of the few Roman works in which physical matters are treated of." It is a collection of natural facts from various writers, Greek and Roman. *Mela* was the author of the first formal treatise on Geography in Latin. He *may* have been the brother of Seneca and the father of Lucan the poet, but this is uncertain. His work was translated into English by Arthur Golding, 1585.

Celsus of the Augustan age wrote eight books on Medicine. *Pliny,* who perished A.D. 79 in the eruption of Vesuvius which destroyed Pompeii and Herculaneum, wrote 37 books on Natural History. This work was translated into English by Holland in 1601. *Solinus* who lived in the third century A.D. wrote a kind of abridgement of Pliny's *Natural History*. His work was much studied in the middle ages and there is an early translation into English—"the excellent and pleasant worke of Julius Solinus Polyhistor containing the noble actions of humaine creatures, the Secretes and Providence of Nature, the description of Countries, the manners of the People, &c., &c., translated out of Latin by Arthur Golding Gent." Lond. 1587.

It will be seen that these authors are chosen not for their style but for their matter, the Latin *words* are only to be used as a means of arriving at *things* expressed by them. Also the concrete knowledge contained in these books is to precede the abstract study of the sciences to which they refer.

P. 12, l. 15. *Enginry*, "engineering."

l. 21. *institutions*, "rules and precepts," compare the *Institutes* of Justinian, an elementary treatise on Roman law.

l. 22. *tempers*, the four temperaments, melancholic, sanguine, lymphatic, choleric. *humours*, the four humours caused the four temperaments, compare Chaucer, "He knew the cause of every maladie, and wher engendred and of what humour." *Seasons*, the effect of the seasons on the health of the body.

l. 23. *crudity*, "indigestion," "constipation."

l. 27. *expenseless*, compare Blackmore, "What health promotes and gives unenvyed peace Is all *expenseless* and procured with ease."

P. 13, l. 3. *commander*, see below, note on page 20.

l. 4. *proceedings*, a university term: we say to *proceed* in law or physic.

l. 12. *natural knowledge*, i.e. knowledge of nature.

l. 16. *facil*, "easy."

Orpheus. The works which have come down to us under the name of *Orphica* are (1) Argonautica, an epic poem in 1384 lines, giving an account of the expedition of the Argonauts. (2) Eighty-seven or eighty-eight hymns, of the Neo-Platonic school. (3) Lithica, a poem treating of the properties of stones both precious and common and their uses in divination. This last poem is undoubtedly alluded to by Milton. *Hesiod.* The *Works and days* is referred to, a poem concerned with the operations of agriculture. *Theocritus* wrote pastoral poems such as Virgil imitated in his *Eclogues. Aratus* wrote two poems on astronomical subjects. Of the writings of *Nicander* two poems remain, *Theriaca*, treating of venomous animals and the wounds inflicted by them, and *Alexipharmaca* of poisons and their antidotes. Under the name of *Oppian* Milton would include two poems, one on fishing *Halieutica*, and the other on hunting *Cynegetica.* They are now known not to be by the same author. *Dionysius* Periegetes, the author of a περιήγησις τῆς γῆς, a general survey of the world as known at that time. How few professed scholars have read the works here enumerated and what a wide grasp of ancient literature they imply!

l. 18. *Lucretius*, the author of the great poem *De rerum natura. Manilius* wrote an astrological poem in five books entitled *Astronomica. Virgil*, the "rural part" would be the *Eclogues* and the *Georgics.*

l. 20. *By this time.* Having spent three or four years in learning the elements of Latin and Greek, mathematics, physics and natural history with the ancient literature that appertains to them, about the age of 15 or 16 they will approach studies which are to form their moral nature.

l. 23. *Proairesis* is the deliberate choice between good and evil in the affairs of life.

P. 14, l. 3. *Plutarch* has been mentioned before, p. 10. There he is to be read to the students in Latin or English, here he is to be studied in the original Greek.

Laertius, Diogenes Laertius the author of a history of philosophy.

l. 4. *those Locrian remnants.* This refers to the treatise ascribed to the Locrian Timaeus, περὶ ψυχᾶς κόσμου καὶ φύσιος. This was printed in a Latin translation by Valla published at Venice in 1488 and 1498 together with other similar treatises.

reduc't, "brought back."

l. 6. *determinate,* "certain," "authoritative."

l. 7. *evanges* = evangels.

l. 10. *Economics.* They are first to learn their duty to themselves and then their duty towards their neighbour.

l. 12. *at any odd hour,* as may easily be done by willing learners, *experto crede.*

l. 15. *comedies,* pictures of social life are to be introduced here, but only a selection, and then with antidote to the possible poison they may contain.

l. 17. *Household matters.* " Euripides the human With his droppings of warm tears, And his touches of things common, Till they rose to touch the spheres."

l. 19. *Politicks,* from the ordering of the house, we rise to ordering the state.

l. 24. *Counsellers.* The statesmen of Milton's age had a difficult task in making up their minds between king and parliament.

P. 15, l. 2. *Licurgus* was the lawgiver of Sparta; *Solon* of Athens; *Zaleucus* of the Epizephyrian Locrians, that is, the Locrians in the South of Italy; and *Charandas* of certain cities in Sicily.

l. 4. *Edicts*, the praetor's edict, the *equity* of Roman law. *Tables*, the laws of the XII. tables. *Justinian* the emperor was the great codifier of Roman law.

l. 10. *at a set hour*, not "at any odd hour" like Italian.

l. 12. *orginal* = original.

l. 14. *Chaldey*, a Semitic language much resembling Hebrew, learnt at Babylon by the Jews in the Captivity. *Syrian*, Aramaic, the ordinary language of Palestine in the time of Christ. We must observe that theological speculation is to be taught concurrently with Politics, the two loftiest subjects which according to Milton's view can occupy the mind.

l. 16. *Histories.* Heroic poem, Tragedies, and Orations are an accompaniment to the study of Politics. Here again are *words* made subservient to *things*.

l. 25. *now lastly*, style and composition is to be taught last of all, the student is not to learn how to write until his mind is stocked with subjects to write about.

l. 26. *organic*, concerned with the use of instruments, "practical."

l. 28. *mean* = medium, the three Latin words would be grande (or excelsum), medium and humile.

P. 16, l. 1. *so much as is useful*, only.

l. 2. *withall*, should be with all.

l. 3. *coucht*, "arranged." *Promptorium Parvulorum*, p. 96, "cowchyn or leyne thinges togedyr, colloco."

Heads and Topics. Heads is a translation of Topics, *Topi*, or the subjects treated of.

l. 4. *contracted palm.* Logic was compared by Aristotle and others to a close fist, rhetoric to an open palm. Cicero *de Finibus*, II. 6. "Zenonis est, inquam, hoc Stoici; omnem vim loquendi, ut jam ante Aristoteles in duas tributam esse partes, rhetoricam palmae, dialecticam pugni similem esse, dicebat, quod latius loquerentur rhetores, dialectici autem compressius."

l. 6. *Phalereus* Demetrius the last of the Attic orators 345—283 B.C. Milton probably refers to the work on elocution which has come down under his name, but which is probably not by him. *Hermogenes* lived about 180 A.D. and did all his work between the ages of 17 and 25. Five works of his are extant which form a complete system of rhetoric.

l. 7. *Longinus* (213—273 A.D.), the author of the well-known treatise on the Sublime; the only one of his numerous works which remains to us.

l. 14. *Horace*, the *ars poetica*.

l. 15. *Castelvetro.* Ludovico Castelvetro wrote among other works *La Poetica di Aristotele vulgarizzata et sposta*, published at Vienna in 1570. See Hallam, *Lit. Europe*, II. 303. 4. *Tasso*, the well-known Italian poet, wrote among his prose works a discourse upon epic poetry and a treatise on poetical composition, and further a dialogue on Tuscan poetry. *Mazzoni's* work *Della difesa della comedia di Dante distinta in sette libri* was published at Cesena in 1587—88. See Hallam, II. 306.

l. 18. *grand master-piece*, the chief point.

l. 21. *comm*, common, the *on* has dropped out, the word perhaps having been written with an abbreviation.

Play-writers. We must not forget that this included Shakespere and the writers of his age.

l. 24. *humane* = human.

l. 28. *fraught*, laden, freighted like a ship.

universal, general. They are not to learn how to compose until their minds are filled with the *things* which they are to write about.

P. 17, l. 2. *Counsel* = council.

l. 5. *then* = than, see above p. 26.

l. 13. *so...as,* a Latin construction expressing a limitation. They are to proceed onward in their studies with this limitation that they are occasionally to go over old ground.

l. 17. *middle ward.* Ward is the same word as guard. We are familiar with vanguard and rearguard in English; a middle ward = middle guard, that is the central body of troops between the van and the rear.

l. 20. *embattelling,* ranging in order of battle. So Shakespere, *Henry V.,* iv. 2, "The highest are embattelled."

P. 18, l. 1. *ancient and famous Schools.* We know little about them.

l. 6. *Studies,* schools or universities. *Cyrene.* Herodotus tells us of a school of physic at Cyrene. Carneades the founder of the new academy came from this city.

l. 12. *the Gown,* the toga, the emblem of peace.

l. 20. *use of their Weapon,* fencing.

P. 19, l. 4. *Gripes.* The verb gripe is to grasp, hold fast; German greifen. *Wrastling,* the middle English for wrestle was wraxlen, wrastlen, or wrasklen, or else wrastle, wraskle, wraxle.

l. 8. *single,* in wrestling they would contend singly one with another. This is in contrast to the combined military exercises mentioned afterwards.

l. 9. *unsweating,* cooling themselves after exercise.

l. 12. *travail'd,* "wearied."

l. 15. *fancied,* full of imagination. *descant* is the harmony which accompanies the plain song or ground subject. *fugues,* compare *Paradise Lost,* XI. 556,

"He looked and saw a spacious plain, wherein
Were tents of various hue; by some were herds
Of cattle grazing : *others, whence the sound
Of instrument that made melodious chime
Was heard, of harp and organ, and who moved
Their stops and chords was seen: his volant touch
Instinct through all proportions low and high
Fled and pursued transverse the resonant fugue."*

l. 16. *Symphony,* a number of musical sounds harmonized together either in the instruments of an orchestra or the stops of an organ. In the English of Milton's time a *symphonist* meant a chorister.

l. 21. *Ditties,* "songs."

l. 27. *concoction,* "digestion."

P. 20. l. 2. *it,* i.e. study.

l. 17. *They would not then...suffer.* My friend Mr S. R. Gardiner whom I consulted on this subject tells me that this passage evidently refers to Essex. "The constant diminution of his army through 1643 from sickness and desertion was a constant subject of complaint, and there was information given to Parliament in the end of that year of companies with only twenty men in them near London amongst those serving under Essex." He also kindly sends me an extract from a despatch of Agostini (the Venetian Secretary) of July 4, 1643, which says that Essex's army was greatly diminished "delle fughe et delle malattie" so that he cannot keep the field without supply. There was talk of deposing him but they feared to do it, "obbligatosi l' Essex i principali commandati suoi con la propria lautissima mensa." This seems to justify "quaff out."

l. 23. *unrecrutible* appears to mean "not able to obtain recruits."

l. 25. *a delusive list, and a miserable remnant*, of the soldiers whose names were on the list only a miserable remnant really existed.

P. 21, l. 15. *year* = years. This was formerly unaltered in the plural, representing a Saxon neuter the same in singular and plural.

l. 19. *commodities*, "advantages."

P. 22, l. 4. *purity*, old English martial prowess coupled with the zeal of a reformed religion.

l. 7. *slight*, here = vile or bad just like its homologue the German *schlecht*.

l. 9. *Kicshoes* is another spelling of *Kickshaws* which means a delicacy or fantastical dish being derived from the French *quelque chose*.

l. 10. *three or four and twenty*. The grand tour is to be taken at this mature age not at 16 or 17. Locke recommends travel at any early age or else deferred until the education is complete. "The time I should think fittest for a young gentleman to be sent abroad would be either when he is younger under a tutor, whom he might be the better for, or when he is some years older without a governor, when he is of age to govern himself and make observations of what he finds in other countries worthy his notice, and that might be of use to him after his return; and when too being thoroughly acquainted with the laws and fashions, the natural and moral advantages and defects of his own country, he has something to exchange with those abroad, from whose conversation he hoped to reap any knowledge."

l. 18.   *other Nations.*   " Italians   might   come   to England for education as Englishmen now go to Italy."

l. 21.   *Diet.*   This is the third great division, and is dismissed in a few lines.

P. 23, l. 10.   *shoot in*, we should say "shoot with."

l. 12.   *Homer gave Ulysses*, when Ulysses returned home after his wanderings.   Penelope offered to give her hand to any of her suitors who could bend the bow of Ulysses.   None could bend the bow except Ulysses himself.

l. 14.   *assay* = essay an attempt.

Cambridge

PRINTED BY C. J. CLAY M.A. AND SONS

AT THE UNIVERSITY PRESS

Cambridge University Press.

Comenius, John Amos, Bishop of the Moravians. His Life and Educational Works, by S. S. LAURIE, M.A., F.R.S.E. 3s. 6d.

Education, Three Lectures on the Practice of. I. On Marking, by H. W. EVE, M.A. II. On Stimulus, by A. SIDGWICK, M.A. III. On the Teaching of Latin Verse Composition, by E. A. ABBOTT, D.D. 2s.

Education, Lectures on the Science of. By FRANCIS WARNER, M.D., F.R.C.P. [*Nearly ready.*

Educational Subjects, Occasional Addresses on. By S. S. LAURIE, M.A., LL.D. Crown 8vo. 5s.

Stimulus. A Lecture delivered for the Teachers' Training Syndicate, May, 1882, by A. SIDGWICK, M.A. 1s.

Locke on Education. With Introduction and Notes by the Rev. R. H. QUICK, M.A. 3s. 6d.

Milton's Tractate on Education. A facsimile reprint from the Edition of 1673. Edited with Notes, by O. BROWNING, M.A. 2s.

Modern Languages, Lectures on the Teaching of. By C. COLBECK, M.A. 2s.

Teacher, General Aims of the, and Form Management. Two Lectures delivered in the University of Cambridge in the Lent Term, 1883, by F. W. FARRAR, D.D., and R. B. POOLE, B.D. 1s. 6d.

Teaching, Lectures on, delivered in the University of Cambridge in the Lent Term, 1880. By J. G. FITCH, M.A., LL.D., Her Majesty's Inspector of Training Colleges. Crown 8vo. New Edition. 5s.

Teaching, Theory and Practice of. By the Rev. E. THRING, M.A., late Head Master of Uppingham School. New Edition. 4s. 6d.

London: C. J. CLAY AND SONS,
CAMBRIDGE UNIVERSITY PRESS WAREHOUSE,
AVE MARIA LANE.

II. LATIN.

Beda's Ecclesiastical History, Books III., IV. Edited with a life, Notes, Glossary, Onomasticon and Index, by J. E. B. MAYOR, M.A., and J. R. LUMBY, D.D. Revised Edition. *7s. 6d.*

———— **Books I. II.** By the same Editors. *[In the Press.*

Caesar. De Bello Gallico, Comment. I. With Maps and Notes by A. G. PESKETT, M.A., Fellow of Magdalene College, Cambridge. *1s. 6d.* COMMENT. II. III. *2s.* COMMENT. I. II. III. *3s.* COMMENT. IV. V., and COMMENT. VII. *2s.* each. COMMENT. VI. and COMMENT. VIII. *1s. 6d.* each.

Cicero. De Amicitia.—De Senectute. Edited by J. S. REID, Litt. D., Fellow of Gonville and Caius College. *3s. 6d.* each.

———— **In Gaium Verrem Actio Prima.** With Notes, by H. COWIE, M.A. *1s. 6d.*

———— **In Q. Caecilium Divinatio et in C. Verrem Actio.** With Notes by W. E. HEITLAND, M.A., and H. COWIE, M.A. *3s.*

———— **Philippica Secunda.** By A. G. PESKETT, M.A. *3s. 6d.*

———— **Oratio pro Archia Poeta.** By J. S. REID, Litt. D. *2s.*

———— **Pro L. Cornelio Balbo Oratio.** By the same. *1s. 6d.*

———— **Oratio pro Tito Annio Milone,** with English Notes, &c., by JOHN SMYTH PURTON, B.D. *2s. 6d.*

———— **Oratio pro L. Murena,** with English Introduction and Notes. By W. E. HEITLAND, M.A. *3s.*

———— **Pro Cn. Plancio Oratio,** by H. A. HOLDEN, LL.D. *4s. 6d.*

———— **Pro P. Cornelio Sulla.** By J. S. REID, Litt. D. *3s. 6d.*

———— **Somnium Scipionis.** With Introduction and Notes. Edited by W. D. PEARMAN, M.A. *2s.*

Horace. Epistles, Book I. With Notes and Introduction by E. S. SHUCKBURGH, M.A., late Fellow of Emmanuel College. *2s. 6d.*

Livy. Book IV. With Introduction and Notes. By H. M. STEPHENSON, M.A. *2s. 6d.*

———— **Book V.** With Introduction and Notes by L. WHIBLEY, M.A. *2s. 6d.*

———— **Books XXI., XXII.** With Notes, Introduction and Maps. By M. S. DIMSDALE, M.A., Fellow of King's College. *2s. 6d.* each.

Lucan. Pharsaliae Liber Primus, with English Introduction and Notes by W. E. HEITLAND, M.A., and C. E. HASKINS, M.A. *1s. 6d.*

Lucretius, Book V. With Notes and Introduction by J. D. DUFF, M.A., Fellow of Trinity College. *2s.*

Ovidii Nasonis Fastorum Liber VI. With Notes by A. SIDGWICK, M.A., Tutor of Corpus Christi College, Oxford. *1s. 6d.*

Quintus Curtius. A Portion of the History (Alexander in India). By W. E. HEITLAND, M.A., and T. E. RAVEN, B.A. With Two Maps. *3s. 6d.*

Vergili Maronis Aeneidos Libri I.—XII. Edited with Notes by A. SIDGWICK, M.A. *1s. 6d.* each.

———— **Bucolica.** By the same Editor. *1s. 6d*

———— **Georgicon Libri I. II.** By the same Editor. *2s.*

———— ———— **Libri III. IV.** By the same Editor. *2s.*

———— **The Complete Works.** By the same Editor. Two vols. Vol. I. containing the Text. Vol. II. The Notes. *[Preparing.*

London : Cambridge Warehouse, Ave Maria Lane.

III. FRENCH.

Corneille. La Suite du Menteur. A Comedy in Five Acts. With Notes Philological and Historical, by the late G. MASSON, B.A. 2s.

De Bonnechose. Lazare Hoche. With four Maps, Introduction and Commentary, by C. COLBECK, M.A. Revised Edition. 2s.

D'Harleville. Le Vieux Célibataire. A Comedy, Grammatical and Historical Notes, by G. MASSON, B.A. 2s.

De Lamartine. Jeanne D'Arc. Edited with a Map and Notes Historical and Philological, and a Vocabulary, by Rev. A. C. CLAPIN, M.A., St John's College, Cambridge. 2s.

De Vigny. La Canne de Jonc. Edited with Notes by Rev. H. A. BULL, M.A., late Master at Wellington College. 2s.

Erckmann-Chatrian. La Guerre. With Map, Introduction and Commentary by Rev. A. C. CLAPIN, M.A. 3s.

La Baronne de Staël-Holstein. Le Directoire. (Considérations sur la Révolution Française. Troisième et quatrième parties.) Revised and enlarged. With Notes by G. MASSON, B.A., and G. W. PROTHERO, M.A. 2s.

—————— **Dix Années d'Exil. Livre II. Chapitres 1—8.** By the same Editors. New Edition, enlarged. 2s.

Lemercier. Fredegonde et Brunehaut. A Tragedy in Five Acts. By GUSTAVE MASSON, B.A. 2s.

Molière. Le Bourgeois Gentilhomme, Comédie-Ballet en Cinq Actes. (1670.) By Rev. A. C. CLAPIN, M.A. Revised Edition. 1s. 6d.

—————— **L'École des Femmes.** With Introduction and Notes by G. SAINTSBURY, M.A. 2s. 6d.

—————— **Les Précieuses Ridicules.** With Introduction and Notes by E. G. W. BRAUNHOLTZ, M.A., Ph.D. 2s.

Piron. La Métromanie. A Comedy, with Notes, by G. MASSON, B.A. 2s.

Racine. Les Plaideurs. With Introduction and Notes, by E. G. W. BRAUNHOLTZ, M.A., Ph.D. 2s.

Sainte-Beuve. M. Daru (Causeries du Lundi, Vol. IX.). By G. MASSON, B.A. 2s.

Saintine. Picciola. With Introduction, Notes and Map. By Rev. A. C. CLAPIN, M.A. 2s.

Scribe and Legouvé. Bataille de Dames. Edited by Rev. H. A. BULL, M.A. 2s.

Scribe. Le Verre d'Eau. A Comedy; with Memoir, Grammatical and Historical Notes. Edited by C. COLBECK, M.A. 2s.

Sédaine. Le Philosophe sans le savoir. Edited with Notes by Rev. H. A. BULL, M.A., late Master at Wellington College. 2s.

Thierry. Lettres sur l'histoire de France (XIII.—XXIV.). By G. MASSON, B.A., and G. W. PROTHERO, M.A. 2s. 6d.

—————— **Récits des Temps Mérovingiens I.—III.** Edited by GUSTAVE MASSON, B.A. Univ. Gallic., and A. R. ROPES, M.A. With Map. 3s.

Villemain. Lascaris ou Les Grecs du XVe Siècle, Nouvelle Historique. By G. MASSON, B.A. 2s.

Voltaire. Histoire du Siècle de Louis XIV. Chaps. I.—
XIII. Edited by G. MASSON, B.A., and G. W. PROTHERO, M.A. 2s. 6d.
PART II. CHAPS. XIV.—XXIV. By the same Editors. With Three Maps.
2s. 6d. PART III. CHAPS. XXV. to end. By the same Editors. 2s. 6d.

Xavier de Maistre. La Jeune Sibérienne. Le Lépreux de
la Cité D'Aoste. By G. MASSON, B.A. 1s. 6d.

IV. GERMAN.

Ballads on German History. Arranged and annotated by
WILHELM WAGNER, Ph.D. 2s.

Benedix. Doctor Wespe. Lustspiel in fünf Aufzügen. Edited
with Notes by KARL HERMANN BREUL, M.A. 3s.

Freytag. Der Staat Friedrichs des Grossen. With Notes.
By WILHELM WAGNER, Ph.D. 2s.

German Dactylic Poetry. Arranged and annotated by
WILHELM WAGNER, Ph.D. 3s.

Goethe's Knabenjahre. (1749—1759.) Arranged and annotated by WILHELM WAGNER, Ph.D. 2s.

———— **Hermann und Dorothea.** By WILHELM WAGNER,
Ph.D. Revised edition by J. W. CARTMELL, M.A. 3s. 6d.

Gutzkow. Zopf und Schwert. Lustspiel in fünf Aufzügen.
By H. J. WOLSTENHOLME, B.A. (Lond.). 3s. 6d.

Hauff. Das Bild des Kaisers. By KARL HERMANN BREUL,
M.A., Ph.D., University Lecturer in German. 3s.

———— **Das Wirthshaus im Spessart.** By A. SCHLOTTMANN,
Ph.D. 3s. 6d.

———— **Die Karavane.** Edited with Notes by A. SCHLOTT-
MANN, Ph.D. 3s. 6d.

Immermann. Der Oberhof. A Tale of Westphalian Life, by
WILHELM WAGNER, Ph.D. 3s.

Kohlrausch. Das Jahr 1813. With English Notes by WILHELM
WAGNER, Ph.D. 2s.

Lessing and Gellert. Selected Fables. Edited with Notes
by KARL HERMANN BREUL, M.A. 3s.

Mendelssohn's Letters. Selections from. Edited by JAMES
SIME, M.A. 3s.

Raumer. Der erste Kreuzzug (1095—1099). By WILHELM
WAGNER, Ph.D. 2s.

Riehl. Culturgeschichtliche Novellen. Edited by H. J.
WOLSTENHOLME, B.A. (Lond.). 3s. 6d.

Schiller. Wilhelm Tell. Edited with Introduction and Notes
by KARL HERMANN BREUL, M.A. 2s. 6d.

Uhland. Ernst, Herzog von Schwaben. With Introduction
and Notes. By H. J. WOLSTENHOLME, B.A. 3s. 6d.

V. ENGLISH.

Ancient Philosophy from Thales to Cicero, A Sketch of. By JOSEPH B. MAYOR, M.A. 3s. 6d.

Bacon's History of the Reign of King Henry VII. With Notes by the Rev. Professor LUMBY, D.D. 3s.

Cowley's Essays. With Introduction and Notes, by the Rev. Professor LUMBY, D.D. 4s.

More's History of King Richard III. Edited with Notes, Glossary, Index of Names. By J. RAWSON LUMBY, D.D. 3s. 6d.

More's Utopia. With Notes, by Rev. Prof. LUMBY, D.D. 3s. 6d.

The Two Noble Kinsmen, edited with Introduction and Notes, by the Rev. Professor SKEAT, Litt.D. 3s. 6d.

VI. EDUCATIONAL SCIENCE.

Comenius, John Amos, Bishop of the Moravians. His Life and Educational Works, by S. S. LAURIE, A.M., F.R.S.E. 3s. 6d.

Education, Three Lectures on the Practice of. I. On Marking, by H. W. EVE, M.A. II. On Stimulus, by A. SIDGWICK, M.A. III. On the Teaching of Latin Verse Composition, by E. A. ABBOTT, D.D. 2s.

Stimulus. A Lecture delivered for the Teachers' Training Syndicate, May, 1882, by A. SIDGWICK, M.A. 1s.

Locke on Education. With Introduction and Notes by the Rev. R. H. QUICK, M.A. 3s. 6d.

Milton's Tractate on Education. A facsimile reprint from the Edition of 1673. Edited with Notes, by O. BROWNING, M.A. 2s.

Modern Languages, Lectures on the Teaching of. By C. COLBECK, M.A. 2s.

Teacher, General Aims of the, and Form Management. Two Lectures delivered in the University of Cambridge in the Lent Term, 1883, by F. W. FARRAR, D.D., and R. B. POOLE, B.D. 1s. 6d.

Teaching, Theory and Practice of. By the Rev. E. THRING, M.A., late Head Master of Uppingham School. New Edition. 4s. 6d.

British India, a Short History of. By E. S. CARLOS, M.A., late Head Master of Exeter Grammar School. 1s.

Geography, Elementary Commercial. A Sketch of the Commodities and the Countries of the World. By H. R. MILL, D.Sc., F.R.S.E. 1s.

Geography, an Atlas of Commercial. (A Companion to the above.) By J. G. BARTHOLOMEW, F.R.G.S. With an Introduction by HUGH ROBERT MILL, D.Sc. 3s.

VII. MATHEMATICS.

Euclid's Elements of Geometry. Books I. and II. By H. M. TAYLOR, M.A., Fellow and late Tutor of Trinity College, Cambridge. 1s. 6d.

Other Volumes are in preparation.

London: Cambridge Warehouse, Ave Maria Lane.

The Cambridge Bible for Schools and Colleges.

GENERAL EDITOR: J. J. S. PEROWNE, D.D.,
DEAN OF PETERBOROUGH.

"*It is difficult to commend too highly this excellent series.*—Guardian.

"*The modesty of the general title of this series has, we believe, led many to misunderstand its character and underrate its value. The books are well suited for study in the upper forms of our best schools, but not the less are they adapted to the wants of all Bible students who are not specialists. We doubt, indeed, whether any of the numerous popular commentaries recently issued in this country will be found more serviceable for general use.*"—Academy.

Now Ready. Cloth, Extra Fcap. 8vo. With Maps.

Book of Joshua. By Rev. G. F. MACLEAR, D.D. 2s. 6d.

Book of Judges. By Rev. J. J. LIAS, M.A.. 3s. 6d.

First Book of Samuel. By Rev. Prof. KIRKPATRICK, B.D. 3s.6d.

Second Book of Samuel. By Rev. Prof. KIRKPATRICK, B.D. 3s. 6d.

First Book of Kings. By Rev. Prof. LUMBY, D.D. 3s. 6d.

Second Book of Kings. By Rev. Prof. LUMBY, D.D. 3s. 6d.

Book of Job. By Rev. A. B. DAVIDSON, D.D. 5s.

Book of Ecclesiastes. By Very Rev. E. H. PLUMPTRE, D.D. 5s.

Book of Jeremiah. By Rev. A. W. STREANE, M.A. 4s. 6d.

Book of Hosea. By Rev. T. K. CHEYNE, M.A., D.D. 3s.

Books of Obadiah & Jonah. By Archdeacon PEROWNE. 2s. 6d.

Book of Micah. By Rev. T. K. CHEYNE, M.A., D.D. 1s. 6d.

Books of Haggai & Zechariah. By Archdeacon PEROWNE. 3s.

Gospel according to St Matthew. By Rev. A. CARR, M.A. 2s.6d.

Gospel according to St Mark. By Rev. G. F. MACLEAR, D.D. 2s. 6d.

Gospel according to St Luke. By Arch. FARRAR, D.D. 4s. 6d.

Gospel according to St John. By Rev. A. PLUMMER, D.D. 4s.6d.

Acts of the Apostles. By Rev. Prof. LUMBY, D.D. 4s. 6d.

Epistle to the Romans. By Rev. H. C. G. MOULE, M.A. 3s.6d.

First Corinthians. By Rev. J. J. LIAS, M.A. With Map. 2s.

Second Corinthians. By Rev. J. J. LIAS, M.A. With Map. 2s.

London: Cambridge Warehouse, Ave Maria Lane.

Epistle to the Ephesians. By Rev. H. C. G. MOULE, M.A. 2s. 6d.
Epistle to the Philippians. By Rev. H. C. G. MOULE, M.A. 2s. 6d.
Epistle to the Hebrews. By Arch. FARRAR, D.D. 3s. 6d.
General Epistle of St James. By Very Rev. E. H. PLUMPTRE, D.D. 1s. 6d.
Epistles of St Peter and St Jude. By Very Rev. E. H. PLUMPTRE, D.D. 2s. 6d.
Epistles of St John. By Rev. A. PLUMMER, M.A., D.D. 3s. 6d.

Preparing.

Book of Genesis. By Very Rev. the Dean of Peterborough.
Books of Exodus, Numbers and Deuteronomy. By Rev. C. D. GINSBURG, LL.D.
Books of Ezra and Nehemiah. By Rev. Prof. RYLE, M.A.
Book of Psalms. By Rev. Prof. KIRKPATRICK, B.D.
Book of Isaiah. By Prof. W. ROBERTSON SMITH, M.A.
Book of Ezekiel. By Rev. A. B. DAVIDSON, D.D.
Book of Malachi. By Archdeacon PEROWNE.
Epistle to the Galatians. By Rev. E. H. PEROWNE, D.D.
Epistles to the Colossians and Philemon. By Rev. H. C. G. MOULE, M.A.
Epistles to Timothy & Titus. By Rev. A. E. HUMPHREYS, M.A.
Book of Revelation. By Rev. W. H. SIMCOX, M.A.

The Smaller Cambridge Bible for Schools.

The Smaller Cambridge Bible for Schools *will form an entirely new series of commentaries on some selected books of the Bible. It is expected that they will be prepared for the most part by the Editors of the larger series (The Cambridge Bible for Schools and Colleges). The volumes will be issued at a low price, and will be suitable to the requirements of preparatory and elementary schools.*

Now ready.

First and Second Books of Samuel. By Rev. Prof. KIRKPATRICK, B.D. 1s. each.
Gospel according to St Matthew. By Rev. A. CARR, M.A. 1s.
Gospel according to St Mark. By Rev. G. F. MACLEAR, D.D. 1s.

Nearly ready.

Gospel according to St Luke. By Archdeacon FARRAR.

London : Cambridge Warehouse, Ave Maria Lane.

The Cambridge Greek Testament for Schools and Colleges,

with a Revised Text, based on the most recent critical authorities, and English Notes, prepared under the direction of the General Editor,

The Very Reverend J. J. S. PEROWNE, D.D.,
DEAN OF PETERBOROUGH.

Gospel according to St Matthew. By Rev. A. CARR, M.A.
With 4 Maps. 4s. 6d.

Gospel according to St Mark. By Rev. G. F. MACLEAR, D.D.
With 3 Maps. 4s. 6d.

Gospel according to St Luke. By Archdeacon FARRAR.
With 4 Maps. 6s.

Gospel according to St John. By Rev. A. PLUMMER, D.D.
With 4 Maps. 6s.

Acts of the Apostles. By Rev. Professor LUMBY, D.D.
With 4 Maps. 6s.

First Epistle to the Corinthians. By Rev. J. J. LIAS, M.A. 3s.

Second Epistle to the Corinthians. By Rev. J. J. LIAS, M.A.
[*In the Press.*

Epistle to the Hebrews. By Archdeacon FARRAR, D.D. 3s. 6d.

Epistle of St James. By Very Rev. E. H. PLUMPTRE, D.D.
[*Preparing.*

Epistles of St John. By Rev. A. PLUMMER, M.A., D.D. 4s.

London: C. J. CLAY AND SONS,
CAMBRIDGE WAREHOUSE, AVE MARIA LANE.
Glasgow: 263, ARGYLE STREET.
Cambridge: DEIGHTON, BELL AND CO.
Leipzig: F. A. BROCKHAUS.

.